THE BLACK DEVILS
AND OTHER POEMS

By
Sterling M. Means

First Fruits Press
Wilmore, Kentucky
c2020

9781648170140

The black devils and other poems
By Sterling M. Means.
Published in the U.S.A. by First Fruits Press, 2020.
Digital version at http://place.asburyseminary.edu/firstfruitsheritagematerial/195

First Fruits Press is a digital imprint of the Asbury Theological Seminary, B.L. Fisher
Library. Asbury Theological Seminary is the legal owner of the material previously
published by the Pentecostal Publishing Co. and reserves the right to release new editions
of this material as well as new material produced by Asbury Theological Seminary. Its
publications are available for noncommercial and educational uses, such as research,
teaching and private study. First Fruits Press has licensed the digital version of this work
under the Creative Commons Attribution Noncommercial 3.0 United States License. To
view a copy of this license, visit http://creativecommons.org/licenses/by-nc/3.0/us/.

For all other uses, contact:

First Fruits Press
B.L. Fisher Library
Asbury Theological Seminary
204 N. Lexington Ave.
Wilmore, KY 40390
http://place.asburyseminary.edu/firstfruits

Means, Sterling M.
   The black devils and other poems / by Sterling M. Means. – Wilmore, Kentucky : First
Fruits Press, ©2020.

   56 pages ; cm.

   Reprint. Previously published: Louisville, KY : Pentecostal Publishing Company,
©1919.
   ISBN: 9781648170140 (paperback)
   ISBN: 9781648170157 (uPDF)
   ISBN: 9781648170164 (Mobi)
   OCLC: 1201304268

   1. African Americans--Poetry. 2. African American Christians--Poetry.   I. Title.

PS2377.M8 B53 2020   814

Cover design by Amanda Kessinger

asburyseminary.edu
800.2ASBURY
204 North Lexington Avenue
Wilmore, Kentucky 40390

First Fruits Press
The Academic Open Press of Asbury Theological Seminary
204 N. Lexington Ave., Wilmore, KY 40390
859-858-2236
first.fruits@asburyseminary.edu
asbury.to/firstfruits

The Black Devils
And
Other Poems

BY

STERLING M. MEANS,
Author of
"The Deserted Cabin and Other
Poems,"
"The German War Lord
and
The British Lion."

PENTECOSTAL PUBLISHING COMPANY,
LOUISVILLE, KENTUCKY.

To the Nine Hundred Thousand Black Troops who fought in France and Flanders this little Volume is respectfully
DEDICATED.

CONTENTS.

THE BLACK DEVILS.

You have read of the French Blue
    Devils,
  How they climb'd the Alpine Peak;
How they fought in France and Flan-
    ders,
  And their deeds like thunder speak;
For they fought with Spartan valor,
  As all history will record,
But they failed to check the Teutons,
  And their raging drunk War Lord;
America calls her Black Devils,
  And lets them loose in the awful
    fray,
They have certainly gone in action,
  They will find 'em hell to play.

They were the first to bear Old
    Glory,
  To the hell-swept Western Front,
Amid the whiz of shells and shrap-
    nels,
  But they bravely bore the blunt.
Big Bertha then was shelling Paris,
  Sending forth her projectiles,

Playing havoc and destruction,
  Throwing her shells a hundred
    miles,
Von Hindenberg's victorious legions,
  Held the Anglo-French at bay,
The Black Devils stormed the center,
  The Germans found 'em hell to
    play.

From the heights of Boston Commons,
  From the battle of New Orleans,
From the stormy days of Richmond,
  To the far off Philippines;
They have fought and fought like de-
    mons,
  For they always win the game;
They have won their country's lau-
    rels,
  From a hundred fields of fame;
As their fathers did yesterday,
  They will do the same today,
They have certainly gone in action,
  They will find 'em hell to play.

BOOKER T. WASHINGTON'S PRAYER.

Lay me down beneath the shadows of
    the long leaf Southern pine,
  Beside the noisy brook and gliding
    stream,
Where the wild honey suckle vine,
Shall around my Tomb entwine,
    And the nights are balmy and fill-
    ed with pleasant dreams.
Lay me down where the S'wanee Riv-
    er waters flow,
  Where the Moon pours its silver
    rays of light,
When I cross the other shore,
In the mystic world I soar,
    Let my parting words to thee, be
    just "Good night."
Lay me down in Dixie where the skies
    are ever blue,
Let me slumber where the sweet mag-
    nolias bloom;
Where the little violets too,
As they drink the morning dew,
    And shed their evening fragrance
    over my Tomb.

(Written in honor of the Colored
Draftees of Indianapolis, who have
gone to the Colors.)

HONEY CHILE, I SAW 'UM PASS.

Did you see our boys a-leavin',
   Ez de bans begin ter play;
An' such a-stepin' to de music,
   Ez dey did on yesterday.

You had to shuv yo' way to see 'um,
   Ez dey marched on to de train,
An' Old Glory she wuz wavin',
   Wid de sound of music strain.

Did you hear de noise an' shoutin',
   Ez dey wuz markin' step by step,
Tho untrained in soldier drillin',
   But wuz flirtin' time wid hep.

Dey stop de cars and blocked de traf-
     fic,
   An' de crowds wuz in a mass,
How did dey look? I can't describe it,
   But Honey Chile, I saw 'um pass.

An' de folks wuz all a-wavin',
  An' little banners filled de air,
Sad "Good byes" and "God be with
      you,"
  While you 'er fightin' "over there."

Dey forgot discriminations,
  Dey forgot dat dey wuz black,
Fur de fires of patriotism,
  Burns in white an' black alike.

Dey will do the deeds of Wagner,
  An' repeat Fort Pillow too,
Where de fathers fought for Free-
      dom,
  In de days of Sixty Two.

But it hab anuther title,
  It iz now Democracy,
Which will mean a higher Freedom,
  When dey fight beyond de sea.

When dey reach de plains of Flanders,
  Dey will face de Germans gas,
An' Brur Kaiser he will tell you,
  Honey Chile, I saw 'um pass.

HAB YOU SEED PHIL BROWN?

Chile, Ise been to Louisville,
   Sent dar ez Delegate,
To 'tend to big Convention,
   Ob old Kentucky State;
Ise a big Republican,
   Knows all erbout politics,
Knows all erbout de Party,
   An' all de cuis trics.
I went to de Pethiam Buildin',
   Soon ez I got in Town,
Some Negroes come an' ax me,
   Why hab you seed Phil Brown?

Great Scots? Who iz dat Negro?
   Iz he a greater man den me?
Hab you heard ob Thacker Lightfoot,
   Ise de second Booker T.
I 'tends all de conventions,
   Ise one ob de leadin' men,
Ise de man you want to see,
   Ef you want your trics to win.
We went to Seelbach Hotel,
   De Biggest House in Town,
When I got dar dey ax me,
   Why hab you seed Phil Brown?

We lef' de Seelbach Hotel,
  And went to Phoenix hill,
An' when dey all had got dar,
  De Negroes wuz axin, still.
De Ban' played, good ole "Dixie,"
  An' "My Ole Kentucky Home,"
But Phil was still de center,
  An' lightning uv de storm.
Soon ez de Ban' had ceased to play,
  An' all had quieted down,
You could hear dem Negroes whis-
     perin',
  Why hab you seed Phil Brown?

Phil wuz sent to Chicago,
  Sent dar ez delegate,
An' who will be next President,
  We all will hab to wait.
An' erbout de War wid Germans,
  I do not fess to know,
An' cannot tell what happen,
  In years ob long ago.
But a thing Ise most nigh certain,
  Will be ax'd in Chicago Town,
Good Morning, Mr. Tedy,
  Why hab you seed Phil Brown?

Should dem Negroes get to heaven,
  An' view de great White Throne,
An' see all de friends an' kinfolks,
  Who now iz dead an' gone.
An' when dey cross de riber,
  Some den would stand an' wait,
To ax de great Saint Peter,
  De keeper at de Gate,
When de Lord sez "Come ye blessed
  To git your starry crown,"
Some Negroes den would ax Him,
  I wonder where iz Phil Brown?

———————

THE LITTLE CABIN NEAR THE PINES.

Tho far from home I've wandered,
  Gone are the distant years,
And the childhood days I squandered,
  Gone are the simple cares;
But they have left an after longing,
  That evoked these measured lines,
Of my Boyhood recollections,
  The little Cabin near the pines.

I have seen many a mansion,
  With ascending frescoed walls,
With their porch of much expansion,
  And their lavish gilded halls;
But they claim no admiration,
  Where the noblest grandeur shines,
As the spot on the Old Plantation,
  The little Cabin near the pines.

I could hear the watch dog howl,
  Thru the stillness of the nights,
And then the noisy owl,
  Would excite my childish frights,
The whippoorwill sung the whole
     night long,
  And would repeat his measured
     lines,
And I still can hear the echo of his
     song,
  As I listen in the Cabin near the
     pines.

THE   KID   FROM   CHATEAU-THIERRY.

The war sho' made a man o' him,
  He was but a slender lad,
When he was called to the colors,
  It left us feeling sad.
But the Kid is now a soldier,
  He has served his country true,
His uniform is the khaki,
  His grand-dad wore the blue.
In the Sixties he was summoned,
  And sent to Harpers' Ferry;
Grand-dad came home from Rich-
      mond,
    But the Kid, from Chateau-Thier-
      ry.

Little did we think when the war
      broke out,
  That the kid would have to go;
And fight four thousand miles away,
  Against a German foe.
And the day he said to us "good-bye,"
  It filled my heart with grief,
Till the tidings came from o'er the
      sea,
    That brought to us relief.

Gone are long and lonesome nights,
  Gone, are the hours dreary,
The boy has come; my heart delights,
  He hails from Chateau-Thierry.

He wears the "Croix de Guerre,"
  For being a gallant lad;
It makes his mother proud o' him,
  And how it pleases dad.
He tells us of his soldier dreams,
  And of the Trench warfare,
And what they meant by "over the
    top,"
  While fighting "over there,"
He is home with us tonight once
    more,
  And let us all make merry,
For the Victor and the Conquered
    foe,
  For the kid from Chateau-Thier-
    ry.

The day he wrote that he would sail,
  I gave his cause to God,
And prayed that he would soon re-
    turn,
  With victory as reward.

The Prodigal son on his return
  From a country far away,
Tho left the paths of righteousness,
  His footsteps went astray.
But his father killed the fatted calf,
  To make the Prodigal merry,
Why, I should shout, rejoice and
      laugh,
  My kid from Chateau-Thierry.

Thank God the war is ended,
  The task we hope is done,
May the fields grow green with clover
  Where Flanders Rivers run;
Our boys have done their duty,
  They were black but valiant men,
And proved as much a soldier,
  As those of fairer skin;
Let America now receive them,
  And her Jim Crowism bury,
For the sake of those who fought
      with him,
  Who hails from Chateau-Thierry.

THE SLACKER.*

We have a slacker in our town,
  He is always on his beat;
You will often find him somewhere
      round,
  The corner of West North Street.
I have never seen him in a store,
  Nor in a Barber shop,
I have never seen him in a row,
  Nor running from a cop.
I have never seen him in a Church,
  Nor at the Y. M. C. A.
I have never heard him sing a song,
  I have never heard him pray.
If you wish to know Brur Josh,
  He has a bread box for his seat,
He sits beside the Market store,
  The corner of West North Street.

I have never seen him in a Park,
  I could not say he shirks,
I have never seen him on a Job,
  I donna where he works.
I have never seen him take a dram,
  I could not say he drinks,

I have never heard him talk enough,
  To find out what he thinks.
His height is far from being tall,
  He is not so very low,
He reminds you of someone you have
      seen,
  In the Southland years ago.
His color is not a sooty black,
  He is far from being brown,
And then he is not what you might
      call,
  The blackest man in town.
Should Gabriel blow the Trumpet
      now,
  He would find a lots in France;
He would find some at the picture
      show,
  He would find some at a dance,
But if he then would find Brur Josh,
  To summon to the Judgment Seat,
He would take the Indiana or River-
      Side Car,
  And stop at West North Street.

———————

* A scene in Indianapolis, suggested
the Poem.

CHRISTMAS TIMES IN SOUTH CAR'LINIA.

I told Sallie to milk de cow,
  While de boys fed de mules;
I recollect twuz Christmas,
  But didn't furget my rules.
My wife Lucy had cooked de cakes,
  An' made some 'lases bread,
I had sold my cotton an' bought my
     gin,
  No need ob actin' dead.
Fur I wuz 'spectin' cumpany,
  From ten miles around dat day.
I had planned to hab sum music,
  To dance de times eway.
Ise uster liberly Christmas,
  An' liberly ain't no sin,
Fur I knowed dey couldn't church me,
  Fur drinkin' a little gin.

It was jest erbout nine o'clock,
  De cumpany wuz gettin' in,
Elder Thacker, my bruder an' hiz
     foks,
  Elder Johnson an' Deacon Wynn.

Well, I met de Elders an' de deacon,
  Told to make demselves at home.
An' dont feel no ways lonesome,
  So we put 'um in anuther room.
Johnny Jenkins comes in wid de ban-
      jo,
  Some one rushed an' told him
Dat de elders an' deacon wuz here,
  Johnny said he had hope to shun
      them
But Christmas comes but once a year.

We served de elders and de Deacon
      'lases cakes,
  An' some good ol' possum meat;
An' dey thanked us very much,
  Fur such a Christmas treat;
Den dey ask dat dey might go,
  In de Room wid de yudder fokst,
Dat dey may hear some moments,
  Ob funny tales and jokes
An' dey said, "'Legion neber wuz de-
      sign
  To make yo' pleasures less,
An' dat wuz de reason dey wouldn't
      be odd,
  F'om de yudder ob de guest."

Let me tell you Honey Chile,
　Some good lookin' gals uz dar;
Some velvet blacks, an' very high
　　　browns,
　Den some wuz mighty fair.
Well, dey line up fur de music,
　Johnny Jenkins touch de strings,
An' hit seem dat de music went all
　　　through you,
　De way he made de banjo ring.

De youngsters begin to cut de capers,
　Begin a-stepin' soft an' slow,
Tell he begin playin' "Down where de
　　　palmettos grow."
　Den ole Ant Lizier goes fur 'lig-
　　　ious,
Took both hands an' closed her ears,
　But her body wuz in motion,
An' her eyes wuz leakin' tears.
　Elder Johnson got so nervous,
Till hiz knee bones gib erway,
　He sed ef "you don't stop dat mu-
　　　sic,
Dat his feet would go astray.
　Ef you don't stop dat dancin',

I will lay my 'legion down,
   Christmas time in South Car'lina,
Will make me lose my starry crown.
   I like to forgot Ant Dinah,
But evahbody knows her,
When Christmas times in South Car-
    'lina.

THE GHOSTS OF EAST ST. LOUIS.

Last night as I lay slumbering upon
    my little couch,
I was questioned, "why Democracy"
    had failed our cause to vouch.
The old Tom Cat was quiet and had
    ceased to chase the mouse;
And a sad majestic silence prevailed
    throughout the house.
The winds were blowing mournfully,
The skies were black with cloud;
And nothing broke the stillness save
    a dog was barking loud.

As I was somewhat nodding and doz-
    ing in a trance,

Dreaming of our soldiers somewhere
 on the fronts in France.
A host of spirits came to me and one
 gave me a gentle touch,
That aroused me in my slumbers and
 disturbed we very much.
The souls of the defenceless, whose
 lives had been robbed;
For they were the helpless victims of
 the East St. Louis Mob.
There were innocent little children,
 mothers, and men giant mould.
They were common rustic toilers
 whose hearts were pure as
 gold.
And they told their solemn mission
 for they had one common plea,
"Will you ask my Country to ex-
 plain Democracy?"

Why, I said that I will tell you or will
 try the best I can.
That true Democracy is the Freedom
 and equal rights of every man.
Then they were more persistent than
 they really were before.

"Please tell us why they mobbed us,
    we would certainly like to
    know?"
"And the murderers go unpunished
    and little is done or said,
When we were simply toiling to earn
    our children's bread."
Then I commence a-weeping as they
    told their Tale of woe,
To think when we are mistreated that
    we had nowhere to go.
All sudden in appearance, came a
    Man of ungainly mould,
"Father Abraham Lincoln with the
    Flag with rippling fold.
He gave fond consolation to the spir-
    its and to me.
He said: "I am the Father and Mar-
    tyr of true, Democracy;
I set the ripple upon the wave and it
    shall break beyond the sea."

THE SOLDIERS AND SAILORS' MONUMENT—INDIANAPOLIS.

Ye Soldiers and Sailors' Monument,
   The splendid shaft from whence it
     rose,
Statues adorned, war implement,
   What deeds of valor they disclose.
Ye Hoosiers' son of rustic toil,
   Thy forms are with the fleeting
     years,
Thy bodies hallowed then the soil,
   In Freedom's cause ye were the
     peers.
Who rent the lightning from the
     cloud,
   And struck with might thy Coun-
     try's Foe,
And tore amid the regal shroud,
   And set the stars of freedom's
     glow.

No polished shaft nor sculptured
     stone,
   Nor epic sung by ancient Bard,

Would now portray what valor won,
  Or bequeath to thee some fond re-
      ward.
Ye were the first to see the light,
  Of liberty's celestial flame,
And taught the world that right was
      might,
    Enshrined it in the halls of fame.
Sleep on, the whole world knows thy
      deeds,
    Lest they forget, we tell the truth,
Thy fame is without minstrel needs,
    It stands a sentinel to the youth.

Ye stalwart, brave heroic men,
  Who came at freedom's high behest,
And thru the shouting and the din,
Found an Empire in the West.
Ye drove the pirates from the seas,
  And put Embargo on thy trade,
Then with thy stern and firm de-
      crees,
    Broke the world's first Blockade.
Ye Soldiers and Sailors' Monument,
  The common heritage of Mankind,
With reverent head and fond content,
  We bow before thy sacred shrine.

Ye broke the Southern bondsmen
  Yoke,
  That made the helpless Black Men
    free;
And thru the flame and battle smoke,
  Ye marched with Sherman to the
    sea.
Ye fought the proud Castilian Foe,
  And broke his scepter in the West,
And drove the tyrant from our door,
  His Empire fell at thy behest.
Ye fought for true Democracy;
  When Freedom's light was like the
    dawn,
And struck to make the helpless free,
  Ere Joffre fought along the Marne.

The unborn youth in after years,
  Shall look to thee with martial
    pride,
To those who bore their Country's
    cares,
  And on the fields of glory died.
No nobler deeds than thine are
    wrought,
  Accept our tribute to thy cause;
The lesson which thy chivalry taught

For nature has no higher laws.
Then thy birthright was divine,
Some battling Seraph led thy way,
And hovered over thy far flung line,
    That bore to us this brighter Day.

WHEN DE WATCH AM RIO GRAN'

Dedicated to the Tenth Cavalry at the
    Battle of Carrizal.

When their captains gave the orders
    For the gallant Tenth to go;
For their troops to cross the River,
    To invade old Mexico;
Then I thought about the Germans,
    And their great embattled line,
When their soldiers went through
        Belgium,
    That they sung: "Die wacht am
        Rhine."
At the Battle of Carrizal,
    With Boyd and Morey in Comman',
Then my muse inspired the lyric,
    That "De watch am Rio Gran."

If some bard should sing the story,
  And would weave a posy spell,
Of the gallant Negro soldier,
  He would have this tale to tell:
That his deeds illumed the pages,
  Of the Golden Book of fame,
Should you read unbiased history,
  You would surely find his name.
He's like Kipling's "Tommy Atkins,"
  "He is a first class fighting man,"
When his captain orders "Forward,"
  And "De watch am Rio Gran."

And they went to death a-smiling,
  With their banner flaunting high,
And they fell but left Old Glory,
  In the breeze of Freedom's sky;
And the ground forever sacred,
  Where the dusky warriors sleep,
And glory is their sentinel,
  While fame their vigils keep.
For the Pass was like Thermopyle,
  But a small heroic Ban',
When they fell at Carrizal,
  When "De watch am Rio Gran."

What's the use of watchful waiting,
  When the awful die is cast,
And the Flag has been insulted,
  And she shudders on her mast,
Listen to the mobilizing,
  Listen to the tramping feet,
Hip-ho ray as now they step it,
  They will never brook defeat,
Listen to the drums a-beating,
  To the music and the Ban',
For the gallant Tenth has told you,
  That "De watch am Rio Gran'"

Tomy Atkins "Tiperary,"
  And the Germans: "Wacht am
    Rhine,"
Will not stir a Negro soldier,
  When he is on the firing line.
When he hears the "S'wanee River,"
  And "My Old Kentucky Home,"
Tho his skin be black as ebon,
  But he is lightning in the storm;
He forgets the cruel treatment
  Of his Race in Dixie Lan'
When its trouble 'long the Border.
  And "De watch am Rio Gran."

THE SOLDIER FAREWELL TO HIS WIFE.

Come kiss me "Good bye," Annie,
    It is time for us to leave,
I have enjoyed your coming,
    We have spent a pleasant Eve.
The transport now is waiting,
    The men are going aboard,
The Captain sends the orders,
    For all we boys to load.
Take good care of the Baby,
    And the other children too,
And may God be with you,
    And you to me be true.

"Keep the home fires burning,"
    And beware of flirts,
Remember a woman's honor,
    Is not in silken skirts.
You must be as true now,
    As you were in maiden life,
Your Husband is now in khaki,
    And you are a soldier's Wife.
Should the little kids annoy you,
    To ask where I am gone,

You must let your face be smiling,
   And do not seem forlorn:
Just sing to them, "America,"
   "My country 'tis of thee,"
The cause for which their father
      fights,
   In lands beyond the sea.

Then you must be a soldier,
   To be a soldier's wife,
To fight on the fronts of honor,
   For a pure and noble life.
The world may not salute you,
   For the victory you may gain,
With the bag pipe and the bugle,
   With the sounds of martial strains.
But the noblest of all the heroes,
   In heaven's high esteem,
Are those who win in battle,
   What the sword could not redeem.
Come kiss me, "Good bye," Annie,
   "Blest be the tie that binds,"
And may our hearts still beat as one,
   When I'm on the firing line.
We'll hold the line along the Marne,
   As the Greeks did Scamander's,
You need not write me darling Wife,
   Till you hear from me in Flanders.

A NIGHT IN FLANDERS.

It was a dark, long lonesome night,
    While we were in the trenches;
We were afraid to use the light,
    Lest we informed the Boches.
I thought of Christ who died for me,
    And spent the Night in Gethse-
        mane.

The shells were bursting thru the air,
    The whole night long,
I thought of Mother's prayer,
    And her old familiar song:
"Dark was the night and cold the
        ground,"
    On which the Lord was found.

Jesus went to Gethsemane,
    To bring Salvation full and free;
I have spent many nights in Flanders,
    For the world's Democracy.
There with the Stars and Stripes un-
        furled,
    I pawned my life to save a world.

I was a sentinel many nights,
  Stood as the Nations guard,
And fought on Armageddon heights,
  For victory and reward.
At Dead Man's Hill I took my
      stand,
  And unfurled the Flag in "No
    Man's Land"

The price I ask for reward,
  Justice and Liberty;
When we conquer the Great War
      Lord,
  Will you remember me;
Will you not my cause despise,
  When you reach Peace-Paradise?

When the Huns within your doors,
  Were but serpents in your breast,
Proved to be your bitter foes,
  But we have stood the test.
We heeded not his propagandas,
  For we fought your foes in Flan-
    ders.

Alll we ask of thee a chance,
  All we ask is a "Square deal"

While we hold the fronts in France.
  Where mighty empires rock and
    reel.
Kill the disfranchising Clause,
  And give us justice in your Law.

Give us Justice at the Bar,
  Will you slay the Serpent Lynch;
And remove the Jim Crow Car?
  While we fight in Flanders trench.
For we are your truest friends,
  We will fight with you till all of it
    ends.

THE ANGEL OF EASTER AND ETHIOPIA.

Angel of Easter, we hail the crimson
    dawn,
The flowers smile with gladness along
    the dewy lawn;
The little feathered songsters are full
    of joy and glee,
The signs of thy presence are seen on
    every tree.

Angel of Easter, Ethiopia prays to
    thee,
That thou mayest bring the tidings
    of true Democracy;
She long has borne the Burden and
    groaned beneath the load;
How long heavenly Messenger, shall
    she totter on the road?
Like the meek and humble Savior,
    her sons are crucified;
In this fair Land of Freedom, their
    rights have been denied.

Those in the courts of Justice, like
    Pilate, have washed their
    hands.
While cruel mobs flayed its victims
    with torch and fire brands.

Angel of Easter, abide with us today,
When trials entomb us to roll the
    stone away,
O may we now entreat thee to tarry
    with us here,
To lift the heavy Burden and to rid
    us of our care.
Thus like the Sainted Jacob, we cling
    now to thy side,
That thou mayest with us linger, and
    still with us abide;
Lo the dark Night is passing; we see
    the light of Dawn,
The resurrected Promise for those
    who fell at Marne.

THE GEORGIA PINE.

Ise longin,' longin' fur de Georgia
    Pine,
An fur dat melon on de melon vine;
An' fur dat sweet brown skin Gal
    o' mine,
An' fur de piney hill,
Where de solumn whipperwill,
Breaks de silence when all iz still,
Save de runnin' brook,
An' de kisses dat I took,
F'om Matilda against her will.
Ise been longin' longin' all de day,
Fur de cotton fields far, far away,
Whur all de good time darkies uster
    stay;
Whur de heart beats ever true,
An' de skies iz always blue,
An' de violets drinks de mornin' dew,
Whur de sweet magnolias bloom,
Fill de air wid its perfume,
Dixie iz Eden made over new.

TO THE ILLFATED TUSCANIA.

"That from these honored dead we
take increase devotion."—Lincoln.

We take increase devotion,
  For the cause for which we fight,
For the cause of every nation,
  Against the German's might;
We stand at Armageddon,
  For the cause which Lincoln stood,
And around the Forts of Verdun,
  Our men have spilt their blood.

We take increase devotion,
  Our Sword shall not return,
Till Freedoms' great salvation,
  On every Altar burn.
Till the rights of every nation,
  Shall be a cause sublime,
Freedom on every ocean,
  In every land and clime.

We take increase devotion,
  And deplore Tuscania's fate,
That sank beneath the ocean,
  To save our Ship of State;

Our noble men who perished,
   Beneath the briny main,
Their memory we shall cherish,
   They have not died in vain.

And when the years are hoary,
   Their deeds, we shall rehearse,
Shall live in song and story
   A Tale of Epic verse;
We take increase devotion,
   For true Democracy,
And we shall do our portion,
   For world wide Liberty.

Behold the Bear of Russia,
   Paralyzed and in the dust,
Struck by the Sword of Prussia,
   A victim of her lust;
Behold the Throne of Belgium,
   They swept her from the earth,
Its nation brought to Serfdom,
   By men of "Kultur" birth.

With the British Lion roaring,
   And almost in his lair,

While France was white from bleed-
    ing,
  And trembling in despair;
Her men which they were routing,
  In trenches filled with gore,
We heard the din and shouting,
  And haste to meet the Foe.

We'll face the Kaiser's mighty guns,
  And hold the Western Line,
And will advance until the Huns,
  Have fled beyond the Rhine.
We take increase devotion,
  As we did on yesterday,
And may the spirit of Lincoln,
  Still lead us on the way.

We have a courage never daunts,
  Nor dreads the Zeplin's notions,
Nor care what submarine that
    haunts,
  The North Atlantic Ocean.
We will fight the Germans anywhere,
  On the land or in the air,
This nation has one constant prayer,
  We take increase devotion.

"THE END OF THE TRAIL."

To Colonel Theodore Roosevelt—
Dead.

I heard the News Boy on the street,
  The words distinctly said,
Crying, "Extra' and then repeat,
  That "Roosevelt is dead;"
The great Man of the "Strenuous
      Life."
Our most illustrious Star,
Had fled this world of war and strife,
  And crossed the mystic bar.
The shocking news which made me
      sad,
  I thought my heart would fail,
The Cartoon which the paper had,
  "It's the end now of the trail."

No more the brave Rough Riders
      charge,
  To advance upon the foe,
Whose fame is with the world at
      large,
  The din and shout are o'er;

The famous Ninth and gallant Tenth,
  Who cut the tangle wire,
With him displayed their fighting
    strength,
  Beneath a rain of fire.
From thence he rose with sudden
    glare,
  The whole world learnt his name,
He rose like Meteor of the air,
  The foremost Son of Fame.

He seeks no more the woolly West,
  To chase the Grizzly Bear;
No more he stirs the eagle's nest,
  Nor the lion in his lair;
No more he lassos on the plains,
  To test the Cow Boys' brand,
With fleeting steed and flowing mane,
  Along the Rio Grande.
No more his touring car shall sweep,
  Along the Western Rail,
The Red man and his tribe shall weep,
  "Its the end now of the trail."

Their "Great White Chief" is laid to
    rest,
  He's laid aside his bow,

He is gone to be the Wigwam's guest,
  Acrost the other shore.
The Black man with his night of
      care,
  Beneath the chast'ning rod,
Would style the great American
      Peer,
  To be "a Chile o' God."
He preached Democracy at home,
  That Justice would prevail,
But he has crossed the surging foam,
  "It's the end now of the trail."

The greatest Man that the world has
      seen,
  Since the days of Christ and Paul,
The man of strong, majestic mien,
  Has heard the solemn call;
The Sage and Prince of Oyster Bay,
  The first Citizen of the world,
Lies a lifeless lump of clay,
  The flag half mast, unfurl'd.
The nations of the earth shall mourn,
  Ethiopia's sons shall wail,
Their truest Friend from earth has
      flown,
  "Its the end now of the trail."

He cut aloose twin Continents,
  To build the great Canal,
The rock-ribbed earth's impediments,
  And all her barriers fell.
He roamed the dark Brazilian wilds,
  And found the River of Doubt,
And the ruins along the banks of
    Nile's,
  He firmly searched them out.
He was the Nimrod of his day,
  The Naturalist and then,
He was the Daniel too to stay,
  In Africa's Lion's den.

He drove his thunderous Car through
    Rome,
  This great American,
Like lightning in the awful storm,
  He shook the Vatican;
When Germany swung her awful
    Sword,
  That caused the dire alarms,
He preached "Preparedness" as code,
  And America rushed to arms.
This mighty Nation heard his voice,
  Was why she did not fail,

He who would've been the Nation's
      choice,
  "It's the end now of the trail."

When Japan with her armies proud,
  Defeat to Russia dealt,
That Rainbow in the Battle cloud,
  Was Theodore Roosevelt;
In Homeland or 'neath alien skies,
  His name is everywhere,
The mother stills her babe who cries,
  With the name of Teddy Bear.
His pen bereft of artful touch,
  He leaves unfinished scroll,
His many books of great research,
  But now we read his soul.

AFRICA AND THE DAWN.

Africa's "Dark land," "Thou ancient
of days,"
Ethiopia's sons stretch forth their
hands,
For the Star of Freedom sends forth
its rays,
Through the wild jungle, crost the
desert's sands;
Thy dark hued children shall now rejoice,
As they hail the dawn of a new
born world,
They shall shout and sing with jubi-
lant voice,
For the flag of Democracy is at
last unfurled.
Thou ancient mother of science and
arts,
Whose civilization with the ages
flown,
Gone, gone are thy cities of opulent
marts,
Thy Rameses the Great, has left his
throne,

Thy fallen temples and shattered
 ruins,
 The pride and the glory that once
  was thine,
Thy rock-hewn chambers and storied
 urns,
 Are more ancient than those of
  Palestine.
Thy history is written in blood and
 tears,
 Two thousand years under Euro-
  pean sway,
Long centuries gray with unending
 cares,
 Now break with the dawn of a
  brighter day.
When the war clouds swung like a
 sable pall,
 And Europe sounded her dire
  alarms,
You heard the thunder and the bu-
 gle's call,
 And sent thy black warriors ar-
  rayed in arms.
They forgot the wrongs which were
 done their race,

With a forgiving heart and defiant
    sword,
And defiant flash from each ebon face,
    They fought the armies of a drunk
        War Lord.
Germany has reaped what she has
        sown;
And the hoarded wealth from Con-
        go's swamps,
Like the chaff of wheat with the
        winds have flown,
    Have all been exhausted in fields
        and camps.
The great God   alone   the Sentinel
        keeps,
    Lest they forget the deeds which
        they have wrought,
Europe in tears her grim harvest
        reaps,
    Its food at the World's Peace Ta-
        ble for thought.

THE GERMAN AFRICAN
COLONIES.

The Slogan, "Africa cannot govern
    herself,"
    Protect her then with "Interna-
        tional Law,"
Take her lambs from the prey of the
    wolf,
    Take her doves from the vulture's
        claw.
'Tis better to leave them with their
    heathen god,
    With whom they have lived three
        thousand years,
Than to give them "Kultur" with a
    bondman's rod,
    And fill their lands with blood and
        tears.

Give them more Christ, less rum and
    creed,
    The glory of the Cross and not the
        flag,

The real Democracy is the thing they
     need,
  From her darkest jungle to her
     highest crag.
Give her cause to the League of Na-
     tions,
  You will see the fruits of her civili-
     zations.
Ye Allied nations with your flags un-
     furled,
  Will you sign the Magna Charter of
     the world?

*THE SONG OF THE KING'S RIFLEMEN.

We er de King's Riflemen,
We fight in de war,
We gwine ter win,
De Germans habe a warrior Chief,
Dun fill de world wid woe an' grief;
His home iz far away Berlin,
His heart is full ob hate an' sin;
We er de King's Riflemen,
We fight in de war,
We gwine ter win,
We er de King's Riflemen,
Riflemen, Riflemen.
We er de King's Riflemen,
We fight in de war,
We gwine ter win.

England knows whut we kin do,
She knows we er soldiers tried an'
        true,
She knows her Zulu warrior will do
        his share,
Fur once we broke de British Square.
We er de King's Riflemen,
We fight in de war,

We gwine ter win,
We er de King's Riflemen,
Riflemen, Riflemen.
We er de King's Riflemen,
We fight in de war,
We gwine ter win,

De fightin' Zulu will neber yield,
Ef we fall on de battlefield;
De white man's God will save us when
      we die,
He lives way up in de sky;
He will open his door an' let us in,
When we tell 'em, we er de King's
      Riflemen.
We er de King's Riflemen,
We fight in de war,
We gwine ter win,
We er de King's Riflemen,
Riflemen, Riflemen.
          Sterling M. Means.

---

*The King's Riflemen of British
Army in South Africa, were mostly
native troops, some white officers.

THE BLACK TROOPS AT THE
BATTLE OF MARNE.*

Ethiopia sends her sons from afar,
  With her rude war song and the
      lance,
To give their lives for the cause
      which they love,
  To die for the freedom of France;
They love her because her freedom is
      real,
  And scorns not the dye of their
      skin;
Their rights are not barred by the
      code of her laws,
  They are treated like citizens and
      men.

The country that treats its subjects
      alike,
  Regardless of color or birth,
Shall live while others shall crumble
      to naught,
  And be swept from the face of the
      earth.

May the future poets and bards of
    thy land,
    Come yet with their tributes of
        thanks,
And sing of their valor that the world
    may know,
    That they fought and fell in thy
        ranks.

The world remembers the fight at the
    Marne,
    That foe they help to repel;
Joffre relates as he orders their
    charge,
    That they rushed like the demons
        from hell.
Von Kluck retreated, his legions fell
    back,
    Before their daring career,
The Crown Prince fainted, was re-
    lieved of command,
    And was borne by his men to the
        rear.

When the powers of might and the
    mail fist shall die,
    That treated the helpless unjust,

Their pride shall perish, their king-
　　doms shall fall,
　Their scepter shall lie in the dust.
When the Teuton is driven beyond
　　their confines,
　And broken his scepter and lance,
The world shall hail thee, O Mother
　　of Arts,
　With the chorus, "Viva la France."
　　　　　　—Sterling M. Means.

———————

　*The French African troops at the
Battle of the Marne helped to turn the
tide of battle; they went into "action"
with their rude war songs and savage
yells; their charge was so exciting
that it unnerved the Crown Prince,
and he was borne by his men to the
rear.

Made in the USA
Columbia, SC
10 October 2023

24232237R00038